LEARN THE ESSENTIAL CHORDS YOU NEED TO START PLAYING JAZZ NOW!

JAZZ GUITAR CHORDS

BY CHAD JOHNSON

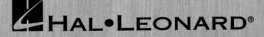

To access videos visit:
www.halleonard.com/mylibrary

Enter Code
8069-2242-9456-7060

ISBN 978-1-4584-0027-7

HAL•LEONARD®

Visit Hal Leonard Online at
www.halleonard.com

Contact us:
Hal Leonard
7777 West Bluemound Road
Milwaukee, WI 53213
Email: info@halleonard.com

In Europe, contact:
Hal Leonard Europe Limited
42 Wigmore Street
Marylebone, London, W1U 2RN
Email: info@halleonardeurope.com

In Australia, contact:
Hal Leonard Australia Pty. Ltd.
4 Lentara Court
Cheltenham, Victoria, 3192 Australia
Email: info@halleonard.com.au

Introduction

Welcome to *Jazz Guitar Chords*. This book will teach you the chords you must know if you want to play jazz. The aim is to get you comping quickly, so we won't get bogged down in too many details. This is not a comprehensive method. Rather, it concentrates on the chord shapes that have stood the test of time and appear in countless jazz songs throughout history.

The chord grids demonstrate each chord with C as the root. However, every chord presented in this book is a moveable form (i.e., there are no open strings used). Therefore, playing these forms from a different root is as simple as sliding them up or down the fretboard. (Refer to the neck diagram in the Appendix for the names of all the notes on the fretboard.)

The seventh chord forms will be shown on four different string groups: 6–4–3–2, 5–4–3–2, 5–3–2–1, and 4–3–2–1. Each of these will also be presented in four forms: root position (root on bottom), first inversion (3rd on bottom), second inversion (5th on bottom), and third inversion (7th on bottom). The remaining chords (extended, altered, etc.) will be shown in several different forms as well, though they will not be presented in as comprehensive manner as the seventh chords. This is because there aren't as many commonly used forms of these. Throughout the book, the root of every chord will be circled. Occasionally, optional notes will appear in parentheses at the top or bottom of a voicing.

After working through this book, you'll be armed with enough chords to work through nearly any jazz song, and you'll have a well-rounded chord vocabulary upon which to build throughout your career. So grab your hollowbody and let's get to swingin'.

About the Video

The video that accompanies this book is a powerful teaching tool. It contains audio/visual examples of every chord covered. The chords are first strummed and then plucked string-by-string, so you can hear each individual note and make sure you've got it right. Also, each example is demonstrated with a full band accompaniment so you can hear these chords in the proper context. In the earlier examples, the chords are played and sustained in a very basic manner so that you can clearly hear the notes. In later examples, the chords are played in more characteristic rhythms. Tuning notes are also included.

Chord grids are provided for many of the examples in the book—especially after a chord type is first introduced—but eventually you'll figure out where they are on your own. The neck diagram in the appendix will be your guide here, but also remember that you can see every chord form used in each video example as well.

Table of Contents

How to Read Chord Diagrams

The chords in this book are presented in chord diagram (or chord grid) fashion. The six vertical lines represent the strings; the lowest pitched (thickest) string is on the left, and the highest pitched (thinnest) is on the right.

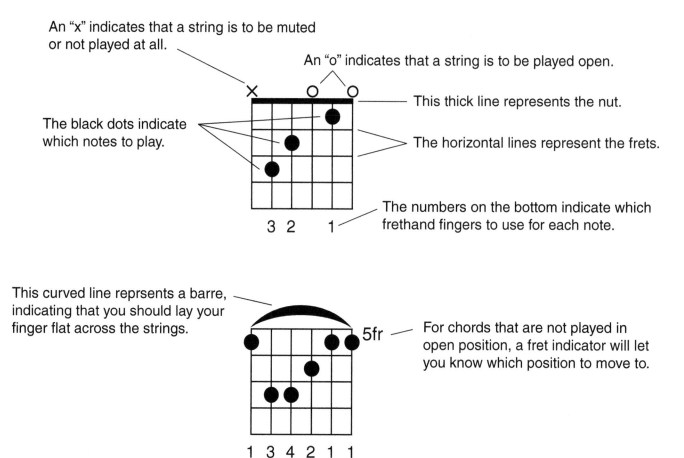

An "x" indicates that a string is to be muted or not played at all.

An "o" indicates that a string is to be played open.

The black dots indicate which notes to play.

This thick line represents the nut.

The horizontal lines represent the frets.

The numbers on the bottom indicate which frethand fingers to use for each note.

This curved line reprsents a barre, indicating that you should lay your finger flat across the strings.

For chords that are not played in open position, a fret indicator will let you know which position to move to.

A Brief Chord Theory Primer

Chords are built from intervals, or degrees, of notes from a major (or minor) scale. A major scale contains seven notes, and those notes are numbered 1 through 7. (The 1 is also commonly referred to as the "root" or "tonic.") So if a chord contains the root, 3rd, and 5th, then it contains the 1st, 3rd, and 5th notes of the root's major scale. If it contains a root, ♭3rd, and 5th, then the 3rd is lowered by a half step. This is referred to as a chord's *formula*. The formula for each type of chord in this book is given.

In order to understand how the chords in this book are built, you simply need to know all twelve major scales, which are found in the Appendix, and apply the formula to a particular root note.

For example, the formula for a major chord is root, 3rd, 5th (or 1–3–5). If you want to understand how a C major chord is built, you would look in the Appendix to find the C major scale. Its notes are C–D–E–F–G–A–B (no sharps or flats). Take the 1st (C), 3rd (E), and 5th (G) notes, and you have the chord. A C major chord is spelled C–E–G.

The formula for a minor chord is 1–♭3–5. So, to build a Cm chord, you would only have to lower the 3rd note (E) down a half step to E♭. So a Cm chord is spelled C–E♭–G. You can use this method to determine the spelling of any chord presented in this book.

A Note on Jazz Rhythm Guitar

Playing rhythm, or "comping" (short for "accompaniment"), in jazz is a bit different than most other genres. Whereas in rock or pop styles, guitarists normally stick to a predetermined riff or chord strumming pattern, jazz guitarists normally improvise their rhythm parts—especially when supporting a soloist. Because of this, it's critical for a jazz guitarist to have quite a large chord vocabulary, enabling him or her to grab a suitable *voicing* (i.e., arrangement of a chord's tones) for a certain chord at any position on the fretboard. Inversions, which will be covered throughout the book, play a significant role in this ability.

The size of the band or ensemble also plays a role in determining the proper voicings to use. If you're playing in a trio with only a bass player and a drummer, you'll more likely be playing chords with more notes than if you're playing in a larger ensemble with five members or more. Most of the chord forms presented in this book can be (and often are) thinned out by omitting notes on top or bottom. For example, the root note is often omitted for a leaner sound, especially when playing with a bassist. Indeed, the great Freddie Green (rhythm guitarist for Count Basie and His Orchestra) often played only one or two notes!

Regarding the right hand, you should experiment with both fingerstyle and using the pick to see which you prefer. It never hurts to be well-versed in both. If you're strumming the chords with a pick, and the notes don't all lie on consecutive strings, you'll need to mute a string with your frethand fingers. This is accomplished by allowing the tip or pad of a finger to contact the adjacent string, thereby deadening it.

With regards to rhythm, things vary quite a bit. Often, guitarists will fluctuate between quick, syncopated (off the beat) chord jabs and long, drawn-out strums that last several beats or more. Ballads generally call for the latter, while upbeat swing tunes may be better suited for the former, though this is certainly not a hard-and-fast rule. *Voice leading* principles are often employed so that the notes of one chord move the least amount possible to reach the next chord.

Most importantly, *listen* to recordings of the genre. There's no more thorough way to get a feel for what works. Besides hearing how the great jazz guitarists (and other rhythm instruments like piano) approach the concept of rhythm, you'll also be getting acquainted with song forms, progressions, etc., all of which are crucial for the well-rounded jazz musician.

SEVENTH CHORDS

Seventh chords are the backbone of jazz harmony. We're going to learn several voicings of many different qualities in this chapter. Again, all of these chords will be presented with a root of C, but you can play them from any root just by sliding them around on the neck. (Refer to the neck diagram in the Appendix for the names of all the notes on the fretboard.)

Major Seventh Chords

The formula for a major seventh chord is 1–3–5–7.

6–4–3–2 String Group

Cmaj7

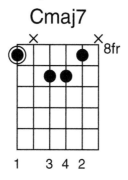

5–4–3–2 String Group

Cmaj7

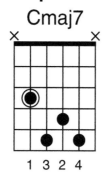

5–3–2–1 String Group

Cmaj7

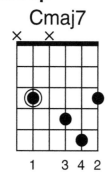

4–3–2–1 String Group

Cmaj7

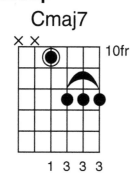

And now let's look at the *inversions* for each of these. An inversion is a chord in which a note other than the root is on bottom. Since seventh chords have four notes, we have three inversion possibilities: first inversion (3rd on bottom), second inversion (5th on bottom), and third inversion (7th on bottom). The first inversion is shown first, followed by the second and third inversions, respectively.

6–4–3–2 String Group

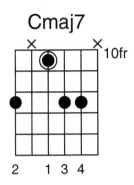

Cmaj7

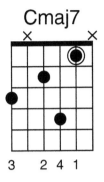

Cmaj7

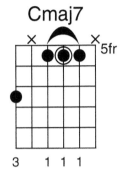

Cmaj7

5–4–3–2 String Group

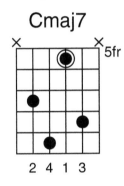

Cmaj7

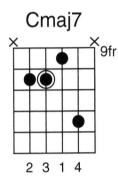

Cmaj7

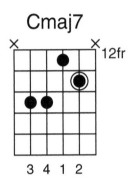

Cmaj7

5–3–2–1 String Group

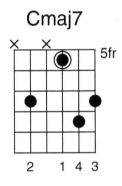

Cmaj7

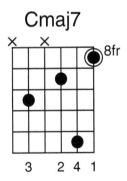

Cmaj7

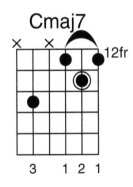

Cmaj7

4–3–2–1 String Group

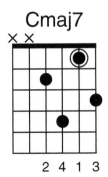

Cmaj7

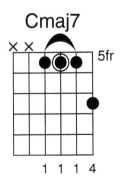

Cmaj7

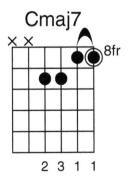

Cmaj7

Minor Seventh Chords

The formula for a minor seventh chord is 1–♭3–5–♭7.

6–4–3–2 String Group

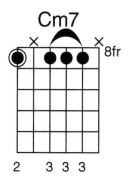

5–4–3–2 String Group

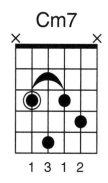

5–3–2–1 String Group

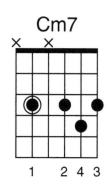

4–3–2–1 String Group

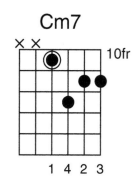

6–4–3–2 String Group

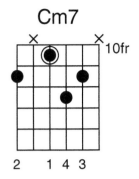

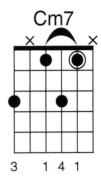

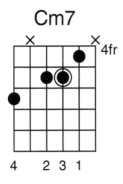

5–4–3–2 String Group

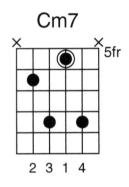

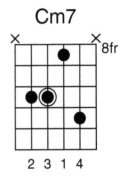

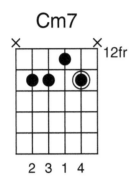

5–3–2–1 String Group

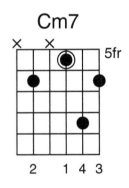

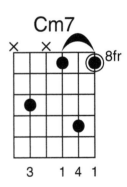

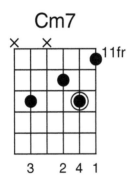

4–3–2–1 String Group

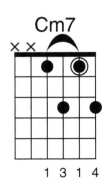

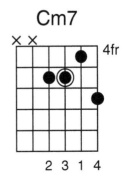

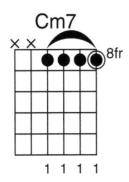

Dominant Seventh Chords

The formula for a dominant seventh chord is 1–3–5–♭7.

6–4–3–2 String Group

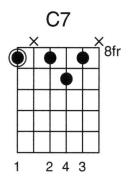

5–4–3–2 String Group

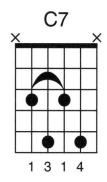

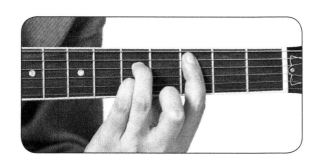

5–3–2–1 String Group

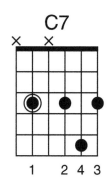

4–3–2–1 String Group

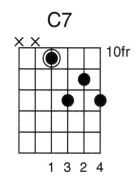

6–4–3–2 String Group

C7
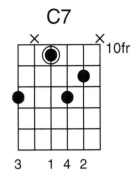

C7
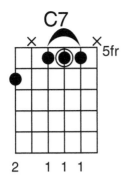

C7
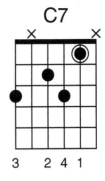

5–4–3–2 String Group

C7
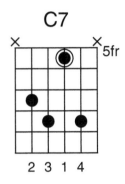

C7
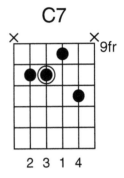

C7
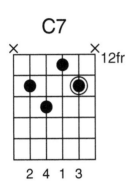

5–3–2–1 String Group

C7
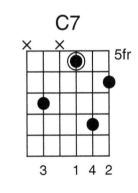

C7
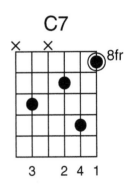

C7
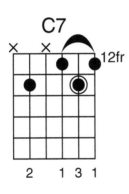

4–3–2–1 String Group

C7
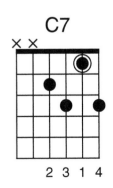

C7
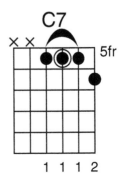

C7
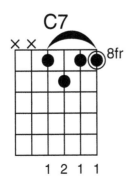

11

You're now armed with enough chords to play some of the most common chord progressions in jazz. This one is a ii–V–I in the key of C: Dm7–G7–Cmaj7.

Example 1

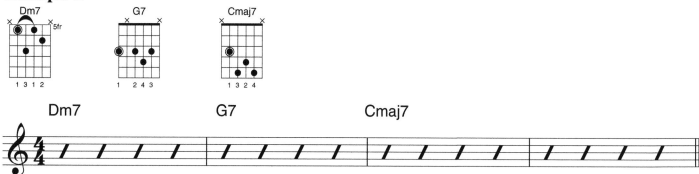

Dm7   G7   Cmaj7

Now here's a ii–V–I in the key of G. We'll be using a different set of voicings for this progression.

Example 2

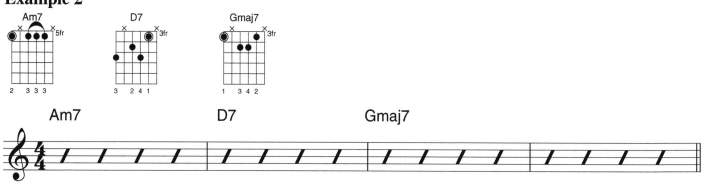

Am7   D7   Gmaj7

And here's another extremely common jazz progression: I–vi–ii–V. We'll play it in D here, which would be Dmaj7–Bm7–Em7–A7.

Example 3

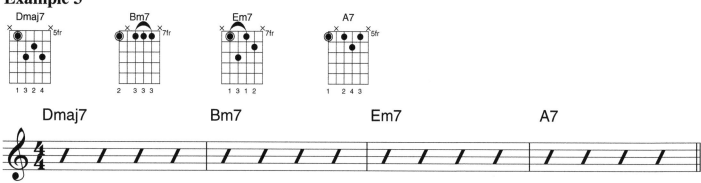

Dmaj7   Bm7   Em7   A7

Often, this progression uses a dominant seventh chord for the VI chord instead of the diatonic vi. We'll play it in D again with this substitution (B7 instead of Bm7). Also, we're using several inversions here so that we're able to remain within a three-to-four fret range of the neck throughout the whole progression.

Example 4

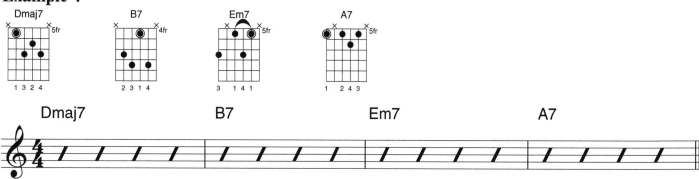

Dmaj7   B7   Em7   A7

Minor Seventh Flat Five (Half Diminished) Chords

The formula for a minor seventh flat five chord is 1–♭3–♭5–♭7.

6–4–3–2 String Group

Cm7♭5

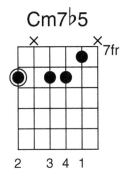

5–4–3–2 String Group

Cm7♭5

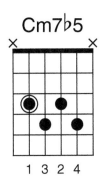

5–3–2–1 String Group

Cm7♭5

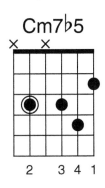

4–3–2–1 String Group

Cm7♭5

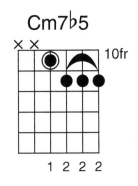

6–4–3–2 String Group

Cm7♭5
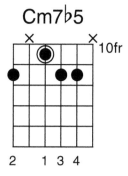

Cm7♭5
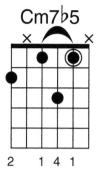

Cm7♭5
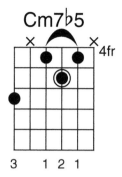

5–4–3–2 String Group

Cm7♭5
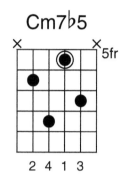

Cm7♭5
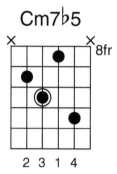

Cm7♭5
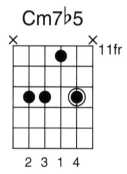

5–3–2–1 String Group

Cm7♭5
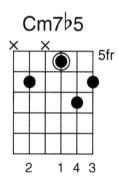

Cm7♭5
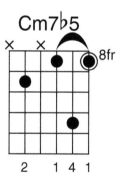

Cm7♭5
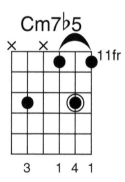

4–3–2–1 String Group

Cm7♭5
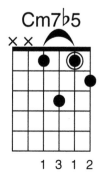

Cm7♭5
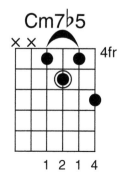

Cm7♭5
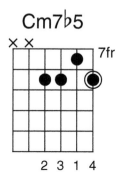

Diminished Seventh (Fully Diminished) Chords

The formula for a fully diminished seventh chord is 1–♭3–♭5–♭♭7.

6–4–3–2 String Group

C°7

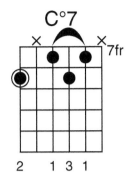

7fr

2 1 3 1

5–4–3–2 String Group

C°7

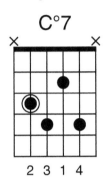

2 3 1 4

5–3–2–1 String Group

C°7

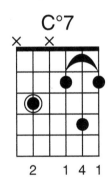

2 1 4 1

4–3–2–1 String Group

C°7

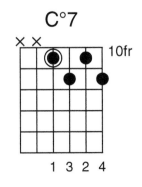

10fr

1 3 2 4

You'll no doubt notice that all these inversions look the same on each string group. This is because the diminished seventh chord is *symmetrical*; it's nothing but four consecutive minor 3rd intervals.

6–4–3–2 String Group

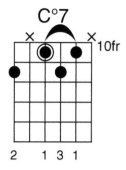

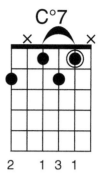

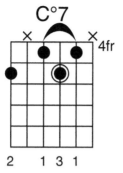

5–4–3–2 String Group

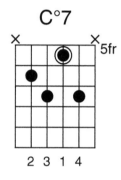

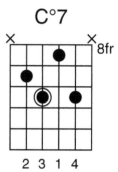

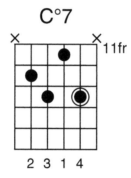

5–3–2–1 String Group

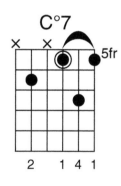

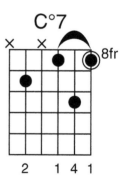

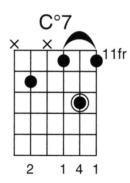

4–3–2–1 String Group

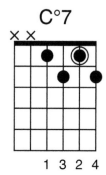

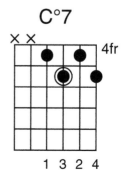

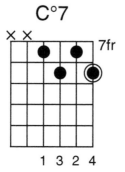

Let's put some of our new chords to work in some more progressions. When we play a ii–V–i in a minor key, the ii chord is half diminished (minor seventh flat five). Here's an example of that in the key of G minor.

Example 5

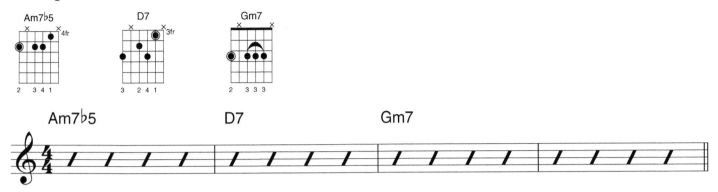

Here's another minor ii–V–i. This one's in the key of D minor and makes use of completely different voicings.

Example 6

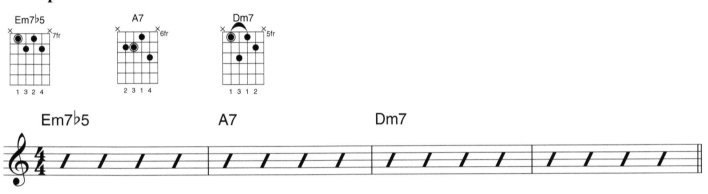

In a I–VI–ii–V progression, it's very common to substitute a diminished seventh chord **built off the ♭II** for the VI chord. This creates a chromatic movement in the bass from the I chord to the ii chord, as shown in this progression in E.

Example 7

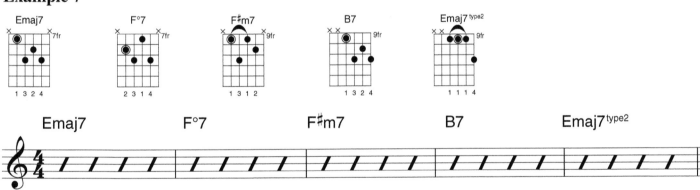

Here's another example of this idea, this time in the key of G major.

Example 8

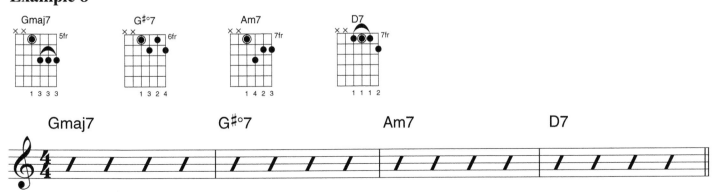

There are two more seventh chord types we're going to look at: minor (major) seventh and seventh suspended fourth. These aren't quite as common as the other seventh chords, so we'll just look at a few different forms for each of them.

Minor (Major) Seventh Chords

The formula for a minor (major) seventh is 1–♭3–5–7.

6–4–3–2 String Group

Cm(maj7)

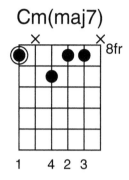

5–4–3–2 String Group

Cm(maj7)

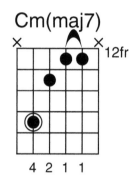

5–3–2–1 String Group

Cm(maj7)

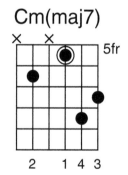

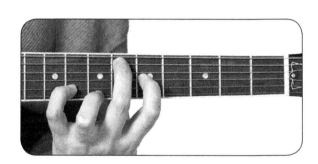

4–3–2–1 String Group

Cm(maj7)

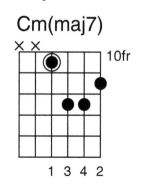

Seventh Suspended Fourth Chords

6–4–3–2 String Group

C7sus4

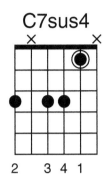

2 3 4 1

5–4–3–2 String Group

C7sus4
3fr

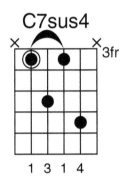

1 3 1 4

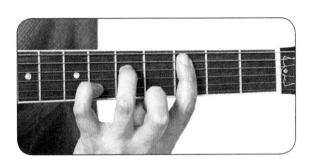

5–3–2–1 String Group

C7sus4
8fr

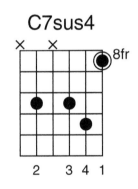

2 3 4 1

4–3–2–1 String Group

C7sus4
5fr

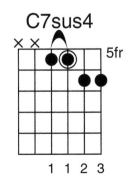

1 1 2 3

Let's play through a few more examples now that make use of all the seventh chord types we've learned thus far. In this example, our V7sus4 (G7sus4) chord substitutes for the ii in a ii–V–I–VI progression in the key of C. (Another name for this G7sus4 chord is Dm11. We'll look at minor eleventh chords later.)

Example 9

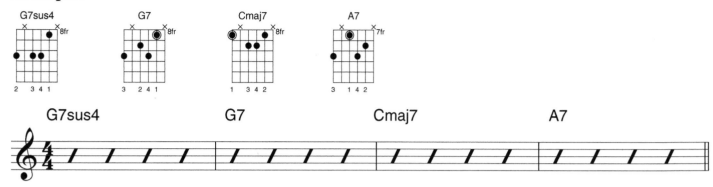

Here we have the first five measures of a jazz blues in the key of D. (We'll look at the complete 12-bar form later in the book.) In measure 4, we're moving to the IV chord (G7) with a ii–V (Am7–D7), but we're substituting D7sus4 for the Am7. (Another name for this D7sus4 chord is Am11.)

Example 10

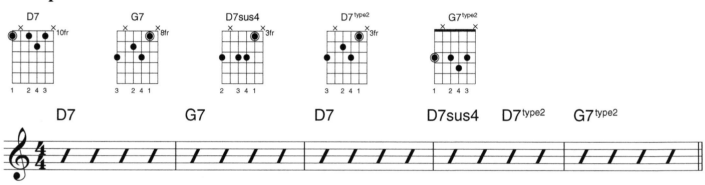

Here we get a look at a typical use for a minor (major) seventh chord: as a passing chord between a minor triad and a minor seventh chord. This progression is in B minor and moves Bm–Bm(maj7)–Bm7–E7, creating a chromatically descending bass line.

Example 11

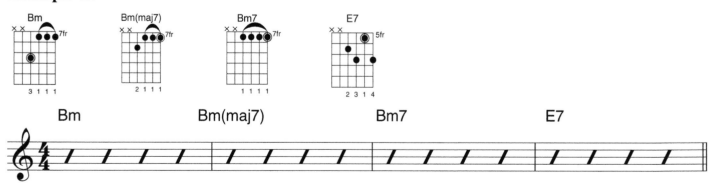

6 AND 6/9 CHORDS

Major or minor 6 and 6/9 chords are common substitutes for major or minor seventh chords. Let's look at a few common voicings.

Major 6 Chords

The formula for the major 6 chord is 1–3–5–6. (The 5th is not always present.)

C6

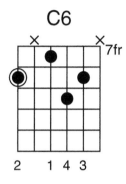

2 1 4 3

C6

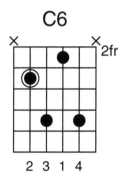

2 3 1 4

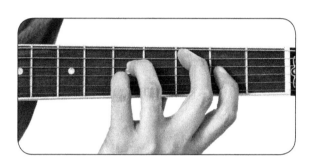

C6

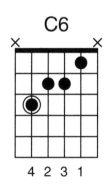

4 2 3 1

C6

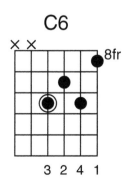

3 2 4 1

Minor 6 Chords

The formula for the minor 6 chord is 1–♭3–5–6. (The 5th is not always present.)

Cm6

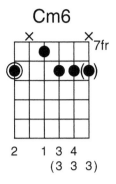

2 1 3 4
(3 3 3)

Cm6

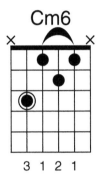

3 1 2 1

Cm6

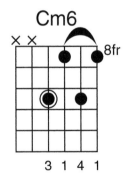

8fr

3 1 4 1

Cm6

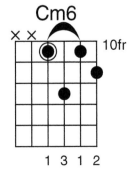

10fr

1 3 1 2

Major 6/9 Chords

The formula for a major 6/9 chord is 1–3–5–6–9. (The 5th is not always present.)

C$^6_9$

5fr

4 1 3 1 1

C$^6_9$

2 1 1 3
(4)

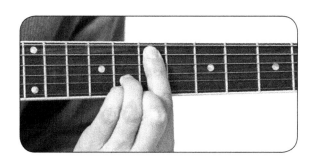

C$^6_9$

7fr

1 1 1 3 4

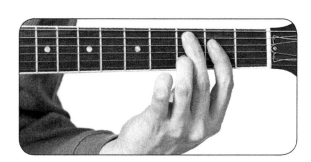

C$^6_9$

9fr

2 1 3 4

Minor 6/9 Chords

The formula for a minor 6/9 chord is 1–♭3–5–6–9. (The 5th is not always present.)

Cm$^6_9$

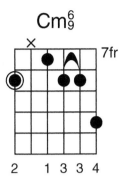

7fr

2 1 3 3 4

Cm$^6_9$

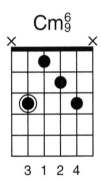

3 1 2 4

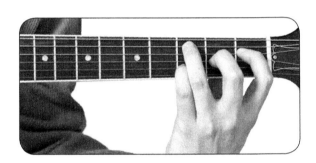

Cm$^6_9$

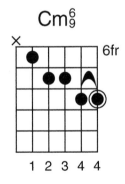

6fr

1 2 3 4 4

Cm$^6_9$

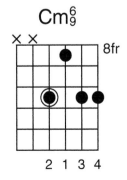

8fr

2 1 3 4

Now let's check out these chords in action. Here's a I–VI–ii–V in B♭ that uses a 6 chord for the tonic (B♭6).

Example 12

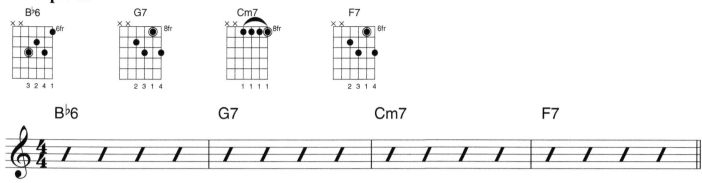

Here we're alternating between seventh chords and 6 chords for the I and ii chords in the key of B: Bmaj7–B6–C♯m7–C♯m6. (The C♯m6 chord here is acting like a rootless F♯9 chord. We'll look at ninth chords in the next chapter.)

Example 13

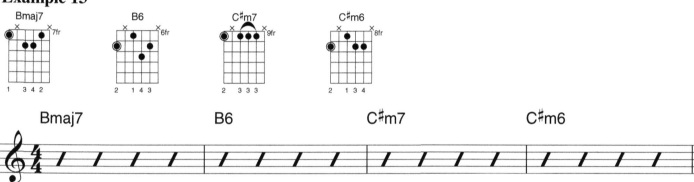

Sometimes 6/9 chords can be moved around for a nice effect, as in this example, in the key of D.

Example 14

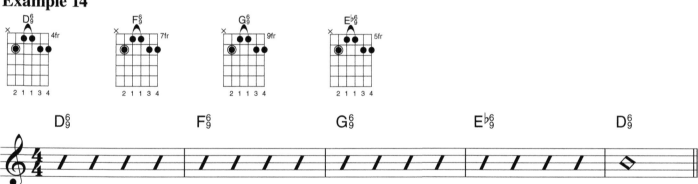

Other times, they can make a great ending chord for an upbeat swing tune. Here's a I–vi–ii–V in the key of A that makes use of both A6 and A6/9 (for the ending).

Example 15

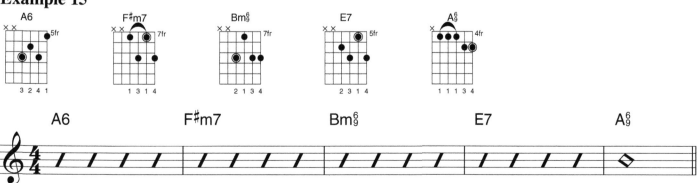

EXTENDED CHORDS

Now let's look at some *extended chords*. Whereas a seventh chord's formula includes the root, 3rd, 5th, and 7th, extended chords keep "stacking 3rds" past the octave. There are three types that we'll look at: *ninth chords*, *eleventh chords*, and *thirteenth chords*. (The 9th degree is the same note as the 2nd, the 11th is the same as the 4th, and the 13th is the same as the 6th, only an octave higher.) Eleventh chords are really only common on guitar as minor elevenths, so we'll just cover those.

Generally speaking, these chords are simply more colorful substitutes for major, minor, or dominant chords. In other words, a major ninth chord can substitute for a major seventh, a dominant thirteenth chord can substitute for a dominant seventh, etc.

Major Ninth Chords

The formula for a major ninth chord is 1–3–5–7–9. (The 5th is not always present.)

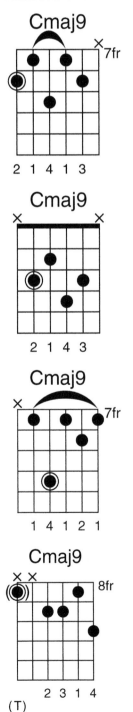

26

Minor Ninth Chords

The formula for a minor ninth chord is 1–♭3–5–♭7–9. (The 5th is not always present.)

Cm9

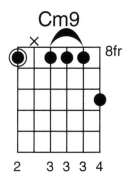

Cm9

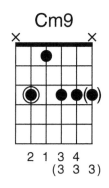

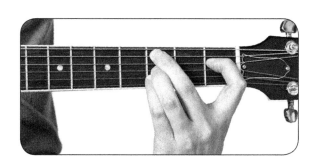

Cm9

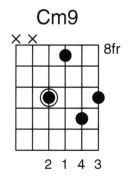

Cm9

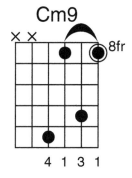

Dominant Ninth Chords

The formula for a dominant ninth chord is 1–3–5–♭7–9. (The 5th is not always present.)

This first voicing is often played as a rootless form, with the sixth string omitted. When the root is included, a barre is employed (shown in the bottom row of fingering).

C9

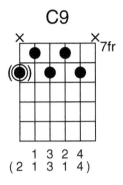

```
1 3 2 4
(2 1 3 1 4)
```

C9

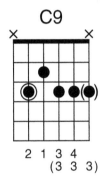

```
2 1 3 4
(3 3 3)
```

C9

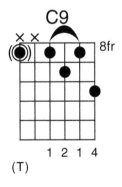

```
1 2 1 4
(T)
```

C9

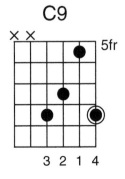

```
3 2 1 4
```

Ninth Suspended Fourth Chords

The formula for a dominant ninth suspended fourth chord is 1–4–5–♭7–9. (The 5th is not always present.)
By the way, if you ever see a chord symbol for a dominant eleventh chord, (G11, for example), you'll do
just fine to play a 9sus4 chord (G9sus4).

C9sus4

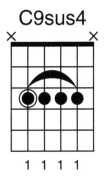

3   4 2 1

C9sus4

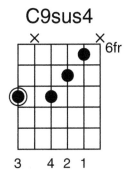

1 1 1 1

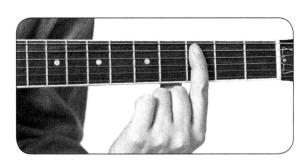

Minor Eleventh Chords

The formula for a minor eleventh chord is 1–♭3–5–♭7–9–11. (The 5th is usually omitted on guitar, as is
often the 9th.)

Cm11

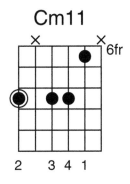

2   3 4 1

Cm11

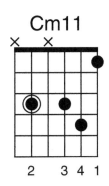

2   3 4 1

Major Thirteenth Chords

The formula for a major thirteenth chord is technically 1–3–5–7–9–11–13, although the 11th is almost always omitted, especially when played on guitar. (The 5th is not always present either.)

Cmaj13

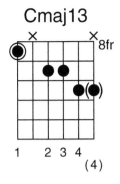

Cmaj13

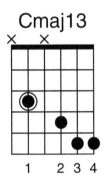

Minor Thirteenth Chords

The formula for a minor thirteenth chord is technically 1–♭3–5–♭7–9–11–13, although the 11th is almost always omitted, especially when played on guitar. (The 5th is not always present either.)

Cm13

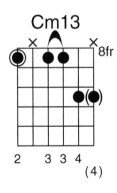

(This voicing is quite a stretch when played low on the fretboard, but it is used often higher up the neck. Therefore, this form is shown in the higher octave.)

Cm13

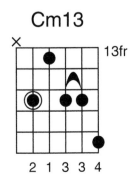

Dominant Thirteenth Chords

The formula for a dominant thirteenth chord is technically 1–3–5–♭7–9–11–13, although the 11th is almost always omitted, especially when played on guitar. (The 5th is not always present either.)

C13

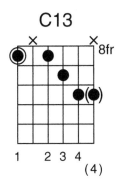

C13

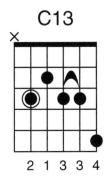

C13

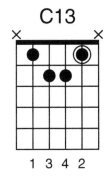

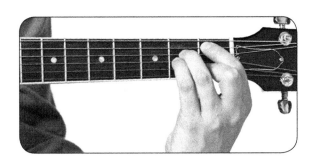

C13

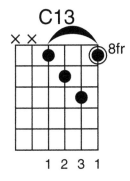

Thirteenth Suspended Fourth Chords

The formula for a thirteenth suspended fourth chord is technically 1–4–5–♭7–9–11–13, although the 11th is almost always omitted, especially when played on guitar. (The 5th is not always present either.)

C13sus4

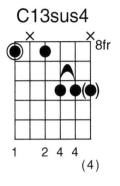

1 2 4 4
    (4)

C13sus4

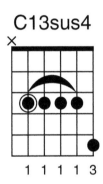

1 1 1 1 3

C13sus4

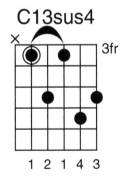

1 2 1 4 3

C13sus4

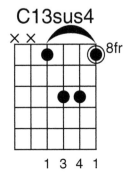

1 3 4 1

Now let's check out how these extended chords sound. Here's a jazz blues in D. Notice the alternate voicing for the final D7 chord. This voicing doubles the root and does not contain a 5th—a fairly common occurrence on seventh chord voicings.

Example 16

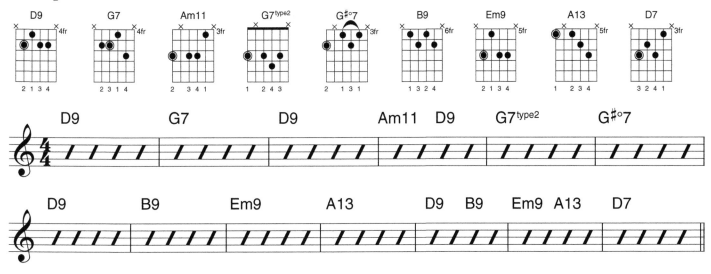

Here's a ii–V–I–VI progression in B♭ that makes extensive use of ninth and thirteenth chords.

Example 17

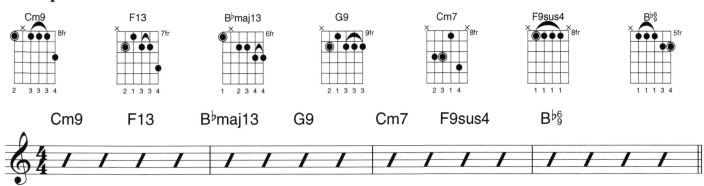

And here's a I–VI–ii–V in A that cycles twice, using different forms each time.

Example 18

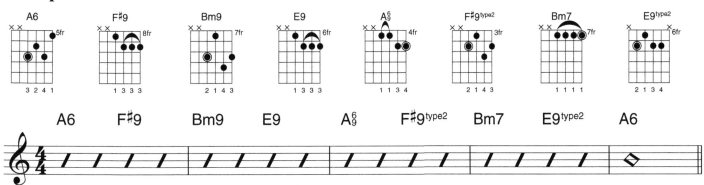

ALTERED DOMINANT CHORDS

An *altered dominant* chord is one in which one or more notes—other than the root, 3rd, or ♭7th—are "altered," or raised or lowered by a half step. (If the root, 3rd, or ♭7th were altered, it would not be a dominant chord anymore.) Altered chords sound quite dissonant or tense and can generally substitute for a standard dominant chord when you want extra tension. We'll look at several common altered seventh, ninth, and thirteenth chords.

Seventh Sharp Fifth Chords

The formula for a seventh sharp fifth chord is 1–3–♯5–♭7.

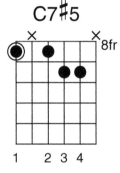

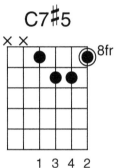

Seventh Flat Fifth Chords

The formula for a seventh flat fifth chord is 1–3–♭5–♭7.

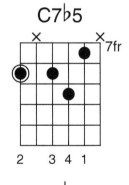

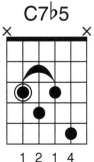

Seventh Sharp Ninth Chords

The formula for a seventh sharp ninth chord is 1–3–5–♭7–♯9. (The 5th is not always present.)

C7♯9

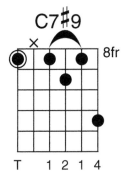

8fr

T 1 2 1 4

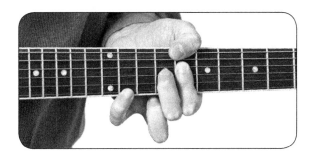

C7♯9

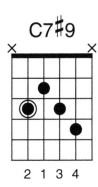

2 1 3 4

Seventh Flat Ninth Chords

The formula for a seventh flat ninth chord is 1–3–5–♭7–♭9. (The 5th is not always present.)

C7♭9

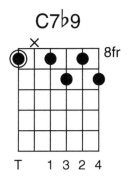

8fr

T 1 3 2 4

C7♭9

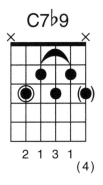

2 1 3 1
(4)

Seventh Sharp Ninth Sharp Fifth Chords

The formula for a seventh sharp ninth sharp fifth chord is 1–3–#5–♭7–#9.

C7#9#5

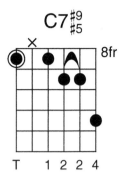

8fr

T 1 2 2 4

C7#9#5

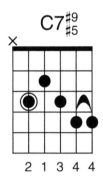

2 1 3 4 4

Seventh Flat Ninth Sharp Fifth Chords

The formula for a seventh flat ninth sharp fifth chord is 1–3–#5–♭7–♭9.

C7♭9#5

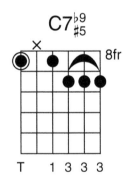

8fr

T 1 3 3 3

C7♭9#5

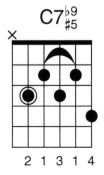

2 1 3 1 4

Thirteenth Sharp Ninth Chords

The formula for a thirteenth sharp ninth chord is 1–3–5–♭7–♯9–11–13, although the 11th is almost always omitted, especially when played on guitar. (The 5th is not always present either.) The second form is root-less, as including the root (shown as empty parentheses) makes the form unplayable.

C13♯9

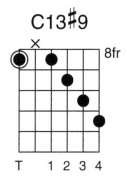

8fr

T 1 2 3 4

C13♯9

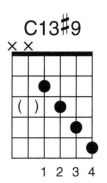

( )

1 2 3 4

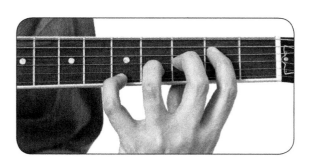

Thirteenth Flat Ninth Chords

The formula for a thirteenth flat ninth chord is 1–3–5–♭7–♭9–11–13, although the 11th is almost always omitted, especially when played on guitar. (The 5th is not always present either.) The second form is root-less, as including the root (shown as empty parentheses) makes the form unplayable.

C13♭9

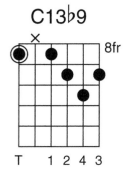

8fr

T 1 2 4 3

C13♭9

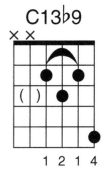

( )

1 2 1 4

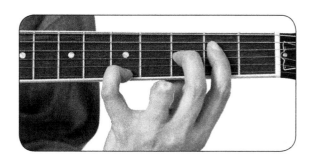

SONG EXAMPLES

Now let's play a few full songs that make use of everything we've covered. The videos will show you which chord forms are used, but feel free to experiment with your own choices for a different sound. We'll be using a few partial voicings here (i.e., we'll omit a note off the top or bottom), so keep an eye out for that.

Example 19

This is a mid-tempo jazz blues in C. Notice that we're using different forms along with some altered dominants in the second chorus. There are dozens of variations on this progression, as there are of the next example as well.

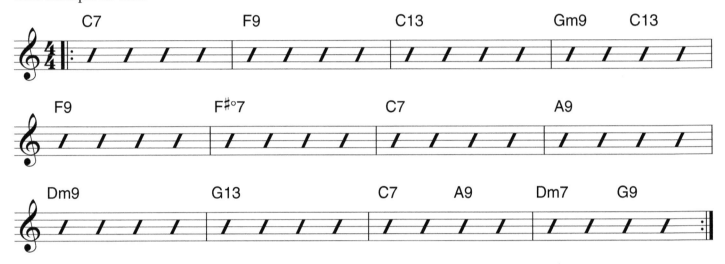

Example 20

Here's a "Rhythm Changes" progression in B♭, based off the chord progression of George Gershwin's "I Got Rhythm." It's a 32-bar AABA form. The tempo of this track is on the slower side for learning purposes, but be aware that most songs based on "Rhythm Changes" are quite brisk. Because of this, smaller, partial voicings are quite common in actual practice.

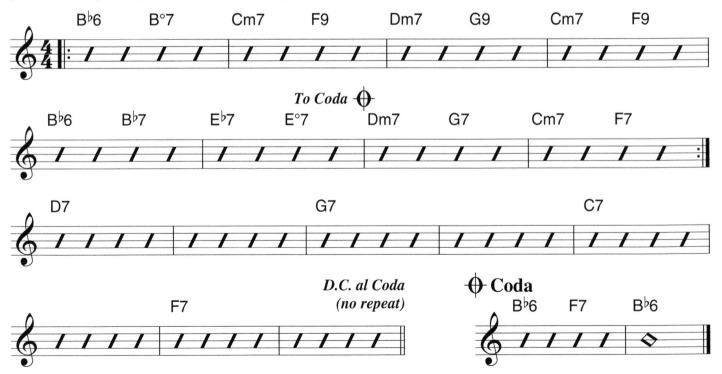

Example 21

This final example is based on another set of common jazz changes. It's played here in the key of A and moves through several different keys. The beginning phrase will give you a workout on your 5-4-3-2 seventh voicings. After that, we begin to incorporate a few more extended chords.

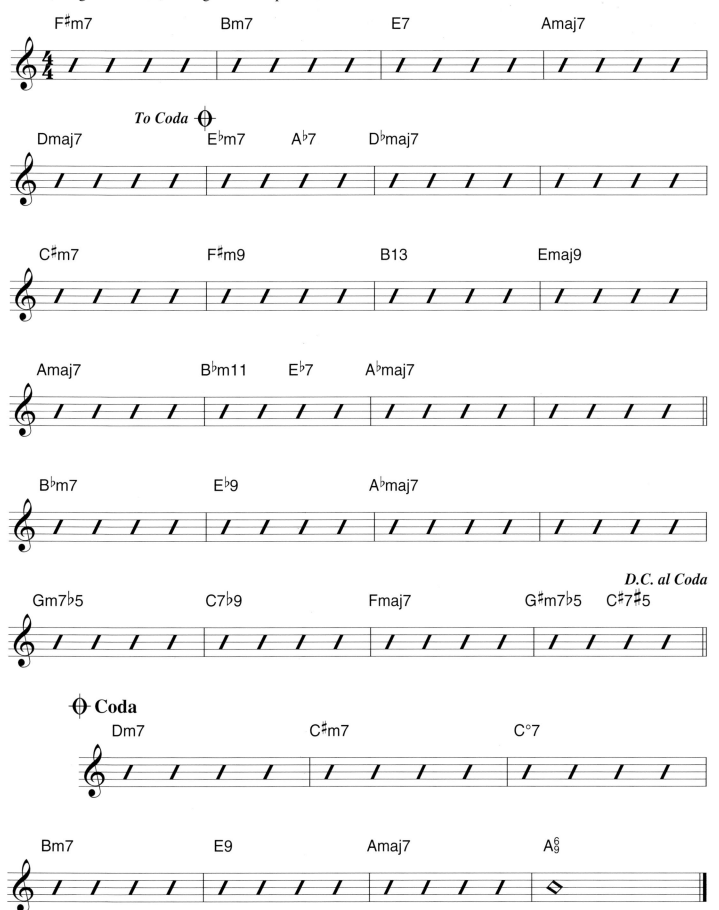

Appendix

Neck Diagram

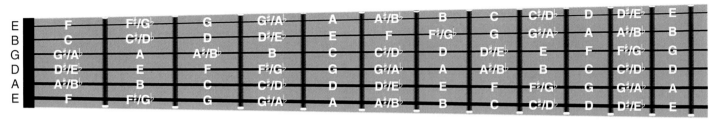

frets: 3   5   7   9   12

Twelve Major Scales

C Major: C–D–E–F–G–A–B

G Major: G–A–B–C–D–E–F$\sharp$

D Major: D–E–F$\sharp$–G–A–B–C$\sharp$

A Major: A–B–C$\sharp$–D–E–F$\sharp$–G$\sharp$

E Major: E–F$\sharp$–G$\sharp$–A–B–C$\sharp$–D$\sharp$

B Major: B–C$\sharp$–D$\sharp$–E–F$\sharp$–G$\sharp$–A$\sharp$

F Major: F–G–A–B$\flat$–C–D–E

B$\flat$ Major: B$\flat$–C–D–E$\flat$–F–G–A

E$\flat$ Major: E$\flat$–F–G–A$\flat$–B$\flat$–C–D

A$\flat$ Major: A$\flat$–B$\flat$–C–D$\flat$–E$\flat$–F–G

D$\flat$ Major: D$\flat$–E$\flat$–F–G$\flat$–A$\flat$–B$\flat$–C

G$\flat$ Major: G$\flat$–A$\flat$–B$\flat$–C$\flat$–D$\flat$–E$\flat$–F

Recommended Listening

Charlie Christian

"Till Tom Special," "Rose Room," "Flying Home"

Freddie Green

"April in Paris," "Corner Pocket,"
"Down by the Riverside"

Wes Montgomery

"Bumpin'," "West Coast Blues," "Four on Six"

Django Reinhardt

"Nuages," "Tiger Rag," "Daphné"

Joe Pass

"'Round Midnight," "All the Things You Are,"
"Blues for Basie"

Jim Hall

"Autumn Leaves," "Alone Together,"
"All the Things You Are"

Kenny Burrell

"Chitlins Con Carne," "Midnight Blue,"
"In a Sentimental Mood"

Barney Kessel

"Louisiana," "(Back Home Again In) Indiana,"
"Time Remembered"

Pat Metheny

"Phase Dance," "Letter from Home,"
"Bright Size Life"